PLACES OF WORSHIP

Mosques

E. Huda Bladon

Heinemann
LIBRARY

First published in Great Britain by Heinemann Library
Halley Court, Jordan Hill, Oxford OX2 8EJ
a division of Reed Educational and Professional Publishing Ltd.
Heinemann is a registered trademark of Reed Educational & Professional Publishing Limited.

OXFORD MELBOURNE AUCKLAND
BLANTYRE IBADAN JOHANNESBURG
GABORONE PORTSMOUTH (NH) USA CHICAGO

Designed by Tinstar Design
Illustrations by Nicholas Beresford-Davies and Martin Griffin
Printed in China by W K T

06 05 04
10 9 8 7 6 5 4

British Library Cataloguing in Publication Data

Bladon, E. Huda
    Mosques. - (Places of worship)
    1.Mosques - Juvenile literature
    I.Title
    297.3'51

ISBN 0 431 05181 X
This book is also available in a hardback library edition (ISBN 0 431 05176 3).

Acknowledgements

The Publishers would like to thank the following for permission to reproduce photographs:
Bladon, Huda, E., p. 17; Emmett, Phil and Val, pp. 5, 8, (top), 11, 13, 15; e.t. archive, p. 8 (bottom); Sanders, Peter, pp. 4, 6, 7, 9, 10, 12, 14, 16, 18, 19, 21.

Cover photograph reproduced with permission of Peter Sanders

Our thanks to Philip Emmett for his comments in the preparation of this book, and to Louise Spilsbury for all her hard work.

Every effort has been made to contact copyright holders of any material reproduced in this book. Any omissions will be rectified in subsequent printings if notice is given to the Publisher.

Contents

Islam and the mosque 4

Different places to pray 6

Inside the mosque 8

Other things to see 10

Who works there? 12

What happens there? 14

Meeting at the mosque 16

Special events 18

Marriage in the mosque 20

Glossary 22

Index 24

Words printed in **bold letters like these**
are explained in the Glossary.

Islam and the mosque

Muslims follow the religion called **Islam**. Islam began in the 7th century in the part of the world we now call the Middle East.

Muslims believe there is only one **God**. Muslims use the **Arabic** word **Allah**. They believe that Allah made everything and everyone.

Most mosques have round roofs called domes.

Muslims often pray in a mosque. Muslims pray facing a place called **Makkah**.

Makkah is important to Muslims because it is where people first worshipped Allah.

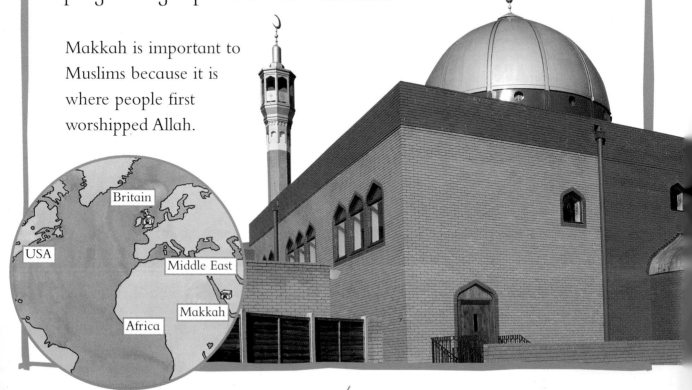

Britain

USA

Middle East

Makkah

Africa

Minarets

Next to the dome of the mosque there is a tall tower or **minaret**. When it is time to pray a man climbs up inside the minaret. He calls out some special words called the **adhan**. This tells Muslims to pray.

The adhan is said in Arabic, not English. Arabic is the language of the **Qur'an**, the Muslim **holy** book. This helps Muslims to feel at home wherever they are in the world.

The minaret is sometimes used to call Muslims to pray in the mosque.

Different places to pray

These Muslims are praying together outside.

Muslims try to think about **Allah** all the time. But there are five special times each day when Muslims pray. It does not matter if they are too far from a mosque because Muslims can pray anywhere that is clean. They can pray at work, in school or even in the street.

The Qur'an

The Muslim **holy** book is the **Qur'an**. In the Qur'an, **God** tells Muslims how to be good. The Qur'an says: 'Everything in the heavens and the Earth belongs to God. All of it **worships** Him.' This shows that Muslims can pray anywhere.

Other places to pray

Sometimes a shop or a house is used as a mosque. Unless you look carefully you may not be able to tell it is a mosque. But even if the outside of mosques look different, inside they are alike.

When Muslim women go to the mosque, they pray in a different room from the men. This is so that everyone can concentrate on Allah while they pray.

Those Muslim women who cannot go to the mosque can pray at home with their children.

Not all mosques look the same outside. This mosque used to be a house.

Inside the mosque

The most important room in a mosque is the prayer room. This is where **Muslims** come to pray. There are no chairs to sit on, but there is always a carpet on the floor. When people are not praying, they sit on the carpet.

Prayer rooms can be very big, like this one.

Prayer mats

Long ago mosques had beautiful rugs on the floor, not one big carpet.

In the prayer room

On one wall of the prayer room, there is a hollow in the wall. It is called the **mihrab**. The mihrab is on the wall closest to **Makkah**. Muslims face this way when they pray.

In most mosques there is a set of special steps called the **minbar**. These steps are used by the **imam** of the mosque. When he climbs up to the top of the steps, everyone can see and hear him.

This Muslim man is sitting in front of the mihrab in this London mosque.

9

Other things to see

Muslims like to make their mosques beautiful. They do this in a special way. The main decoration is **Arabic** writing copied from the **Qur'an**. This writing can be made into beautiful patterns and it helps people to remember **Allah**.

There are no pictures or statues inside a mosque. This is to help people to think only of **God** and the Qur'an while they are in the mosque.

These words remind Muslims of Allah.

Places to wash

Every mosque has a place to wash because Muslims have to wash before they pray. This special washing is a way of showing respect and care for Allah.

It also gives Muslims a time to get ready to think about Allah.

No one must walk in the mosque with shoes on or the carpet will get dirty. There are special racks to put your shoes in.

This is the place where Muslims do the special washing (called **wudu**) before praying.

Who works there?

One man is usually in charge of the mosque. This is the **imam**. The imam often calls the **adhan**, which tells people that it is time to pray. He may also lead the prayers inside the mosque. He is chosen to be imam because he knows a lot about **Islam**.

The imam tries to help **Muslims** in lots of ways. He may answer their questions about the best way to live. He might also help with family problems. He is a busy man so sometimes he has people to help him.

The imam leading the prayer in a mosque in Chesham.

Other people

Some Muslims come to the mosque to clean it. The mosque is where people pray, so it must always be very clean.

It is important that the mosque is kept clean at all times.

Big mosques collect money to give to poor people. Muslims from the mosque go to visit the poor and give them money. They do this in their spare time.

What happens there?

The mosque is a very busy place. There are always people there. Prayers are held in the mosque five times a day, and many **Muslims** like to go to the mosque to pray with other people.

The times of prayer are written in the **Qur'an**. The first one is before sunrise, when it is still dark. The last prayer is at night. Muslims who live near the mosque may come for every prayer.

These Muslims have just finished praying the late evening prayer, the last of the day's five prayers.

Mosque school

Most mosques have a school where Muslim children learn about **Islam**. They go every night after normal school. They may also go on Saturdays and Sundays. First they learn the **Arabic** letters. Then they can learn to read the Qur'an. When they are older they have other lessons about Islam.

These children are learning to read Arabic so that they will be able to read the Qur'an for themselves.

Meeting at the mosque

Friday is a special day for **Muslims**. All the men and boys go to the mosque. Before the midday prayer the **imam** gives a speech called a **khutbah**. In it he may talk about something in the news or about a problem to do with **Islam**. After the prayer the men talk to each other. Then they go back to work.

This imam is giving the speech before the Friday prayer in a mosque in Norwich.

Study in the mosque

All Muslims have to learn about Islam. They meet together to learn from someone who knows more then they do. They learn to read and understand the **Qur'an** properly. Muslim women have their own groups.

These women are learning about Islam.

Finding answers in the mosque

Many people come to the mosque to find out answers to questions they have about Islam. Many mosques have study rooms or libraries with books to help people. Some of the bigger mosques even have bookshops where Muslims and others can buy books and copies of beautiful **Arabic** writing.

Special events

Every year there is a special month for **Muslims** called **Ramadan**. In this month, Muslims do not eat or drink anything during daylight hours. They try to think about **Allah** more than usual and be especially good.

Every evening when it is time to eat again, Muslims meet up with each other. They might go to a friend's house or the mosque. After they have eaten a little they pray the evening prayer. Then they have a proper meal before praying special Ramadan prayers.

Muslims try to break their **fast** at the end of a Ramadan day in their local mosque.

Id

After Ramadan there is a festival called **Id**. Children have a day off school and new clothes to wear. In the morning Muslims go to the mosque to pray.

After the Id prayer the rest of the day is spent visiting friends. Muslims may also give cards and presents to each other on this special day.

Many Muslims celebrate Id with parties, especially for children.

Sweets for Id

Muslim children like eating special sweets at Id. Try making some yourself. Take the stones out of some dates. Ask an adult to cook the dates slowly with a little water until they form a soft paste. When this is cold you can make it into balls. Lastly, roll the balls in some chopped nuts, such as walnuts.

19

Marriage in the mosque

When a **Muslim** man and woman want to get married they often go to the mosque. In front of the **imam** or other mosque leader they show that they want to get married.

They do this by deciding on a set of things about their marriage which they put in a **contract**. This may include where they will live and what presents the man will give his wife. The imam talks to them about the importance of caring for each other.

This Muslim man and woman are signing their marriage contract.

The wedding celebration

After a couple are married, there are usually two big parties. All the men and boys go to one party. The women and girls have a party for themselves, and the bride is beautifully dressed. The mosque itself may be used for very big wedding parties.

After the ceremony, guests at a Muslim wedding enjoy a feast.

Glossary

adhan (a-than) special words said from the minaret to call Muslims to pray

Allah (al-la) the Arabic word for God

Arabic the language of the Qur'an and Muslim prayer. All Muslims know some Arabic, some speak it all the time.

contract a written agreement, in this case of the decisions a Muslim man and woman make when they get married

fast to go without food or drink, usually because of your religion

God Muslims believe God made, sees and knows everything. Muslims call God Allah, the Arabic word for God.

holy means respected because it is to do with God

Id (ee-d) the name for a festival or holiday in Islam. There are two Ids every year. One is at the end of Ramadan.

imam a Muslim man who leads the prayers

Islam the religion of Muslims. Muslims believe in one God, called Allah in Arabic. They also believe a man called Muhammad was special because he was the last man on Earth to have messages from God.

khutbah (kut-ba) the speech given by the imam during Friday and Id prayers

Makkah a town in Saudi Arabia. There is a very old mosque there called the Ka'bah, which Muslims believe to be the place where Allah was first worshipped. All Muslims face Makkah when they pray.

mihrab (mih-rab) a decorated area of one wall in the prayer room of a mosque. This is the wall closest to Makkah.

minaret the tall tower next to a mosque. It is used to call Muslims to pray.

minbar (min-bar) special steps in a mosque used by the imam on a Friday to speak to the Muslims

Muslim person who follows the religion of Islam

Qur'an (kor-an) the book given by God to Muhammad

Ramadan (rum-a-than) a month of the Islamic year. Muslims fast in this month.

worship to show respect and love for God or Allah

wudu the special washing Muslims do before prayer

Index

adhan 5, 12, 22

Allah 4, 6, 7, 10, 11, 18, 22

Arabic 5, 10, 15, 17, 22

dome 4

fasting 18, 22

holy books 5, 6

Id 19, 22

imam 9, 12, 16, 20, 22

Islam 4, 12, 15, 16, 22

khutbah 16, 23

libraries 17

Makkah 4, 9, 23

marriage 20, 21

Middle East 4

mihrab 9, 23

minaret 5, 23

minbar 9, 23

Mosque schools 15

prayer 4-5, 6-7, 8-9, 12-13, 18-19

prayer mats 8

prayer room 8-9

prayer times 14

Qur'an 5, 6, 10, 14, 15, 17, 23

Ramadan 18, 23

washing (wudu) 11, 16, 23

women 7

worship 6, 23